Birth and Early Years of Gandhiji's Life

Mahatma Gandhi is one of the most revered names in Indian history. He was the political and ideological leader of India, also honoured as Father of our nation, he became an international symbol of the free India. He played a very important role in the Indian freedom movement. He is lovingly called as Bapu. His teachings of 'Ahinsa' and 'Satya' (non-violence and truth) changed the complete outlook of the Indian freedom fighters.

Mohan Das Karamchand Gandhi, also known as Mahatma Gandhi, was born on 2nd October 1869 in a Hindu family of Porbandar, Gujarat. His parents were Karamchand Gandhi and Putlibai.

His father, Karamchand Gandhi was a Diwan (Chief Minister) of Porbandar and an honourable and upright man. Gandhiji's mother was a religious and pious woman. Gandhiji gained high moral and social values from his parents. Since childhood, Gandhiji believed strongly in non-violence, truth, purity and very simple lifestyle.

At the age of 13, Gandhiji got married to a girl of the same age named, Kasturba Gandhi. They had four sons. Gandhiji started his education in Porbandar. He further studied in Rajkot and did his matriculation. Then, he joined the University of Bombay in 1887. His family wanted him to become a barrister.

In 1888, he went to London for further studies and completed his law in 1891. He returned to India. For the next two years, he practised law in India.

Gandhiji in South Africa

At the age of 23, Gandhiji left his family once again and came to South Africa as a legal advisor of an Indian businessman. In South Africa, Gandhiji found that there was a strong demarcation between the Black and White communities. The Black community faced a lot of discrimination and were very badly treated. Gandhiji felt very bad about this.

Just after a week of his stay, Gandhiji experienced the humiliation because of discrimination. One day, he had to travel in a train. He had a first-class ticket with him. At the Pietermartizburg station when he entered the first-class compartment and was asked to shift to the third-class compartment. The ticket checker told him that the first-class was reserved for Whites.

On raising objection on this discrimination, Gandhiji was thrown out of the train.

During this journey, he late came to know that discrimination is the common practise there. The Black community and the Indians were called 'coolies'.

After this incident, Gandhiji decided to fight against this injustice. He wrote letters to the higher officials and began a protest against the discrimination in South Africa.

For the next three years, Gandhiji continuously fought for the justice. Soon, he became a well-known activist and a leader of the Indian community.

On 22nd May 1894, Gandhiji established an organisation—Natal Indian Congress (NIC) in South Africa. This organisation looked after the rights of Indians living there. While working for NIC, Gandhiji also faced a lot of opposition from the other communities. He was also attacked several times.

Gandhiji spent twenty years in South Africa. Thereafter, in the year 1915, he returned to India.

Gandhiji in India

Gandhiji's struggles and successes in South Africa were well known in India also. He became a 'National Hero' in the eyes of Indians. Gandhiji wanted to create the same wave of reformation in India. He travelled to all the parts of India to know the real conditions of Indians.

While his travels, Gandhiji used to wear a dhoti and wooden slippers. He renounced all the pleasures and adopted a very simple lifestyle.

He established the 'Sabarmati Ashram' in Ahmedabad, Gujarat. He lived in the ashram with his family and some of his supporters. Everyone loved and supported Gandhiji.

People started believing in his teachings of non-violence and truth. He got the title of 'Mahatma', which meant 'a great soul'.

The Indian Freedom Movement

India was under British rule at that time. A large number of freedom fighters were fighting for the freedom of India. Gandhiji also wanted the freedom of India but he followed a different path. He began a non-violent movement called 'Satyagraha' against the British.

Satyagraha means opposition, but not in an aggressive form. Gandhiji taught people to ask for justice in a silent way. The movement created a strong wave and became a great success.

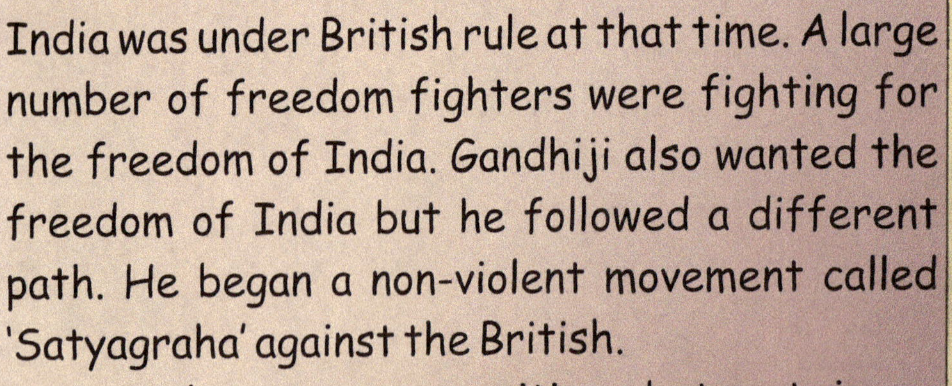

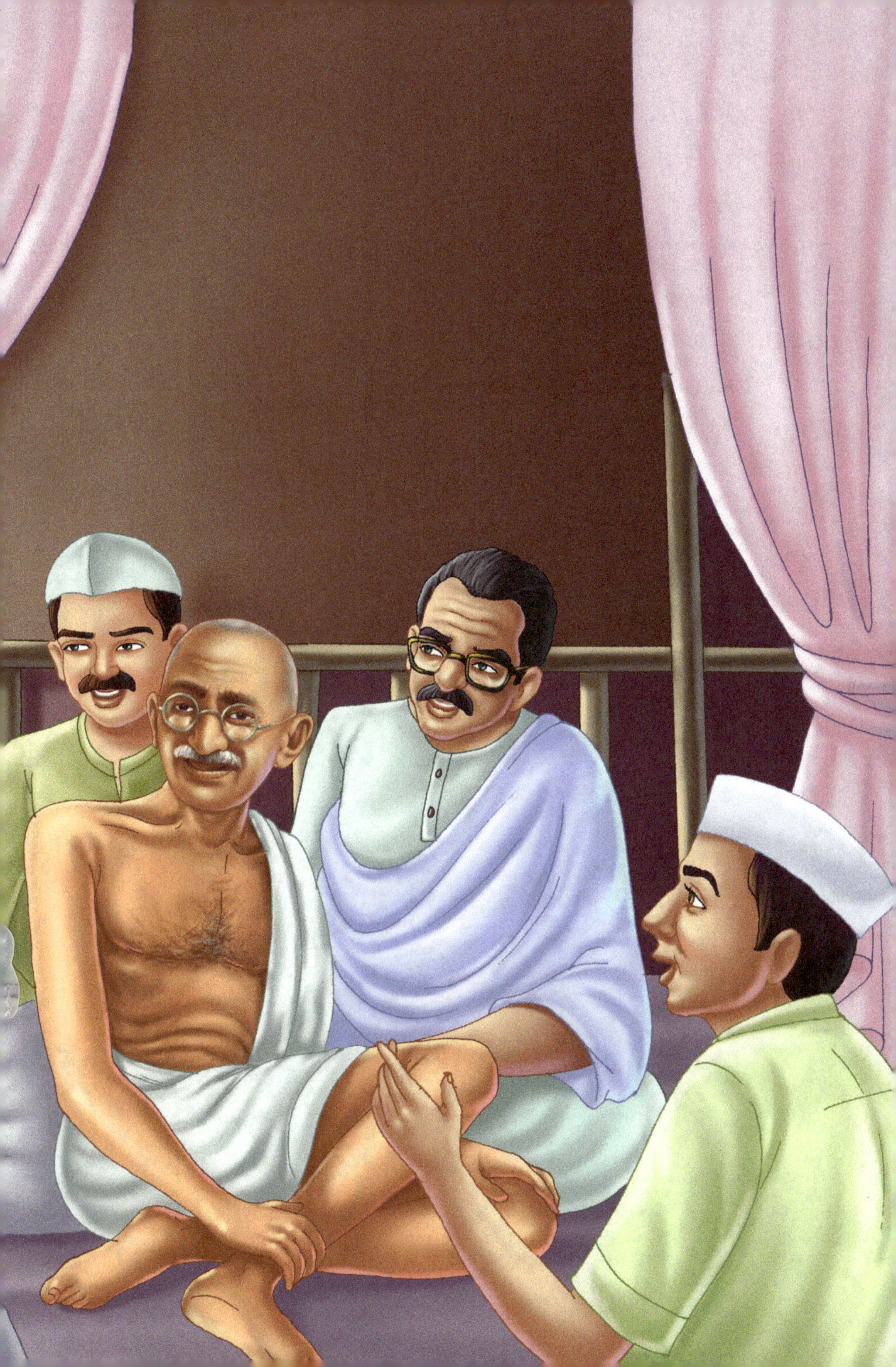

In 1919-20, Gandhiji started another movement called 'Non-cooperative movement'. During his struggle for freedom, Gandhiji was sent to jail many times by the British Govt, but he continued his mission. He asked indians to stop using foreign clothes and other things. He insisted to spin natural cloth on Charkha (spinning wheel). The image of the Charkha later became a symbol of the Indian independence.

On 12th March 1930, Gandhi ji began 'Dandi March' or the 'Salt March' against the salt tax. Gandhi ji with his supporters stand walking 200 miles from Sabarmati Ashram towards the sea.

On April 5, the group reached Dandi, a place along the Coast. Gandhiji demonstrated the method to make salt from the seawater. Soon, the movement spread in the entire nation. Gandhiji was imprisoned once again but, the protest continued nationwide. It was stopped only after the 'Delhi Pact' between the British Government and Gandhiji. The Pact granted the limited salt production and all the protestors were released.

In 1942, Gandhiji issued the last call for independence from British rule. He initiated another movement called 'August Kranti.' Soon after, he began 'Quit India' movement that asked the Britishers to leave India.

After the long struggle and sacrifices, India became independent on 15th August 1947. At the time of freedom, India faced the partition in two parts. After the freedom, Gandhiji tried to maintain peace and unity among the people of different communities.

There was a lot of disturbance in all the parts of country. The communal violence was spreading fast. To stop this violence, Gandhiji began a 'fast unto death' on 13th January 1948 which proved to be a success. On 18th January 1948, he ended his fast only when he got the assurance that the communal violence would be stopped.

Assassination of Gandhiji

Some Indians believed that Gandhiji was responsible for the partition of India. Gandhiji faced a lot of opposition.

On the unfortunate day of 30th January 1948, Gandhiji was going to address a prayer meeting. He was walking along with his two assistants—Abha and Manu. Just when he was stepping towards the stage to address the public, a man named Nathuram Godse fired at Gandhiji.

Gandhiji fell on the ground, saying, "Hey Ram, Hey Ram!" These were the last words of Mahatma Gandhi.

The great soul, the light of the nation, was gone. The whole country was mourning bitterly on their dear Bapu's departure from the world. The other countries were also shocked at his death.

Soon after the assassination of Mahatma Gandhi, Pt. Jawahar Lal Nehru addressed the nation on radio:
"Friends & Comarades, The light has gone out of our lives and there is darkness everywhere. I do not know what to tell you and how to say it. Our beloved leader, Bapu as we called him, the Father of the Nation, is no more.
Perhaps I am wrong to say that. Nevertheless, we will never see him again as we have seen him for these many years. We will not run to him for advice and seek solace from him, and that is a terrible blow, not only to me, but also to millions and millions in this country.
And it is a little difficult to soften the blow by any other advice that I or anyone else can give you.."

India Remembers Mahatma Gandhi

Mahatma Gandhi's Samadhi is at Raj Ghat in Delhi. Thousands of people from all over the country come to Raj Ghat to pay homage to the great man.

2nd October, Gandhiji's birthday is celebrated as 'Gandhi Jayanti'. It is one of the three National festivals of India. People of India still remember their dear 'Bapu' with great love and reverence.

Every year, 30th January—the day of Gandhiji's assassination, is observed as the Martyr's Day to commemorate the struggle of all those who sacrificed their life for the country. Mahatma Gandhi's picture is also printed on the Indian currency notes.

Mahatma Gandhi was a great writer also. He wrote and edited many newspaper articles during his lifetime. He also wrote several books including his autobiography— My Experiments with Truth.

In the year 1930, Time magazine named Mahatma Gandhi as 'The Man of the Year'. There are many books written about him and his teachings. The life of Mahatma Gandhi has been widely portrayed in the Indian literature, theatre and movies.

Mahatma Gandhi dedicated his entire life for the welfare of Indians. He has been the greatest source of inspiration for all the Indians. His teachings of non-violence, peace and truth are still practised and followed by many, not only in India but also in other countries.

The only way to pay tribute to the great man—The Father of Our Nation—is to follow his teachings in our lives. We should learn from the great life of Mahatma Gandhi.

India's Hope: Narendra Modi

The land of Gujarat has produced many talented person who added to the glory of Gujarat and India. Shri Narendra Modi is also one such person, often addressed as the 'Gujarat's Development Man'. His life-story is full of struggles and hardships yet quite inspiring one as well. Nowadays the acronym of his name, 'Namo' (Narendra Modi) has become an inspiring mantra not only in the country but abroad as well for the majority of Indians.

Family and Childhood

Narendra Modi was born in Vadnagar, a small town in north Gujarat, in Mehsana district, on 17th Sept. 1950. His complete name is Narendra Damodardas Modi. His father's name is Damodardas Moolchand Modi and his mother is Hiraben Modi. His parents have six children and he is their third issue. His elder brothers are Somabhai and Amritbhai and two younger ones are Prahlad and Pankaj. His only younger sister is Vasantiben. His father, Damodardas, used to run a tea-stall near the office of a former Congress leader, Rasik Bhai Dave.

Financially his family was quite hard-pressed. Although Narendra Modi passed his childhood in utter penury, he never allowed the poverty influence his life in anyway. He would merrily swim in a river flowing nearby his home and enjoy his life in the company of his friends. Plucking off the raw mangoes from a closely mango-orchard was his favourite and the naughtiest prank.

Even at this age he had begun to appear quite thoughtful, and endowed with a foresight as well. What grieved most his young heart was the prevalent social evils like untouchability and injustice due to casteism. He equally abhorred discrimination practised against the women-folk. Depicting the agony of a Dalit woman he wrote a play called 'Peela Phool' (the yellow flower) in which he also played a role when it was staged.

Education and Development

Child Narendra was admitted in the primary school of Vadnagar. Like an obedient son he regularly attended his classes. But he has an inborn urge to do something different, something extra-ordinary. He completed his education upto 10th class in the Bhagwataacharya Narayanaacharya Higher Secondary School. In 1967 Modi went to Visanagar for his intermediate education. Owing to his friendly attitude he developed a lot of friends among whom he was popularly known as 'ND' (the initials of his full name- Narendra Damodardas).

But whenever he saw his father working at the tea-stall, he felt quite disturbed. The longing to rise high and achieve something distinct was germinated at this very juncture. After his school hours he would invariably come to the tea-stall to help his father. Many a time he would himself accompany his father to the Vadnagar Railway Station to sell tea with him. At times he even sold water bottles and personally carried the oil-filled canisters of the oil companies. When he became young, the religious faith or Dharm had a distinct impact on him. For him Dharm meant social service and elimination of evils from the social ethos. He also emphasized on the spiritual aspect of Dharm. He keeps fast twice in a year during Navaratri festivals. He get internal strength from the fast.

Political Leadership

Right from his student life the quality of leadership had begun to show its effect which made him very popular. His readiness to help his fellow students in their hour of need and the capacity to guide them further honed up his leadership quality. Now he had started taking interest in the political happenings which not only inspired him but also made him become a source of inspiration for others. His belief was: 'he who thinks high and acts to fulfill his high aspirations eventually moves on the path of progress'.

His capacity to analyse the events and their consequences became his strength. When he faced any problem, first he would like to satisfy himself with its possible solution before guiding others. These qualities of him made him emerge as the leader of the Akhil Bhartiya Vidyarthi Parishad (ABVP).

He also served as the Pracharak of the RSS at various stations. But he had no desire to join politics. His only mission was spreading the thoughts and ideology of the Sangh. It was for this purpose, he joined 1974's 'Navnirman Andolan' , an agitation against corruption and came in the lime-light. In this phase, he got ample opportunity to learn the subtlety of politics. Meanwhile, continuing his studies, in 1980 he did his M.A. in Political Science from the University of Gujarat. In 1984, it was decided to include all the Sangh Pracharaks into the BJP. Looking at Modi's dedication, he was made a member of the BJP which heralded the beginning of his political career. In 1988, he was made the General Secretary of the State's BJP unit. Later on he was made the National Secretary of the BJP.

Tourism and Environment

Right from the childhood, Modi has abiding interest in Nature and environment. He loved swimming and could merrily swim across the Sharmishtha Lake, undaunted by its bubbling waves. He also loved visiting new places and seeing new sights. When he joined the RSS he got many more opportunities to behold Nature closely and understand its secrets. He would visit Ramakrishna Mission and Vivekananda Ashram in Almora. In 1972, he got an opportunity to travel picturesque Kangra as the Pracharak of RSS. He also wanted to stay for long in the Ramakrishna Mission in Belur Math but couldn't due to his other commitments. He specially visited Vivekananda Ashram of Almora perhaps in his attempt to follow the great seer's life principles. He also visited Kailash Mansarovar where he experienced much internal peace but he had to return soon owing to his father's demise.

Even before becoming the CM of Gujarat, Narendra Modi never neglected tourism because he knew the importance of environment and Nature. In 2001 when Modi took the charge as the CM, the State was recovering from the damages it underwent due to the massive earthquake. His government completed the Earthquake Rehabilitation Programme only in 8 months' time. The victims were properly rehabilitated and a campaign was launched to make people harvest rain water and meet their water demands. This campaign was admired globally and the World Bank awarded Gujarat with the 'Green Prize'.

Energy Power

After becoming the Gujarat CM, Gujarat's development became the new centre-point of Mr. Modi's ambitions. He stipulates the Panch Varsheeya Yojana (The Five Year Plan) which had five parts: Knowledge power, Energy power, Hydro power, People's power and the Fighting power (Rana-Shakti). This unprecedented plan proved very effective eventually and gave an impetus to Gujarat's progress which was based on Narendra Modi's original thinking and good management. All these powers encouraged the urban development plans in a tremendous way.

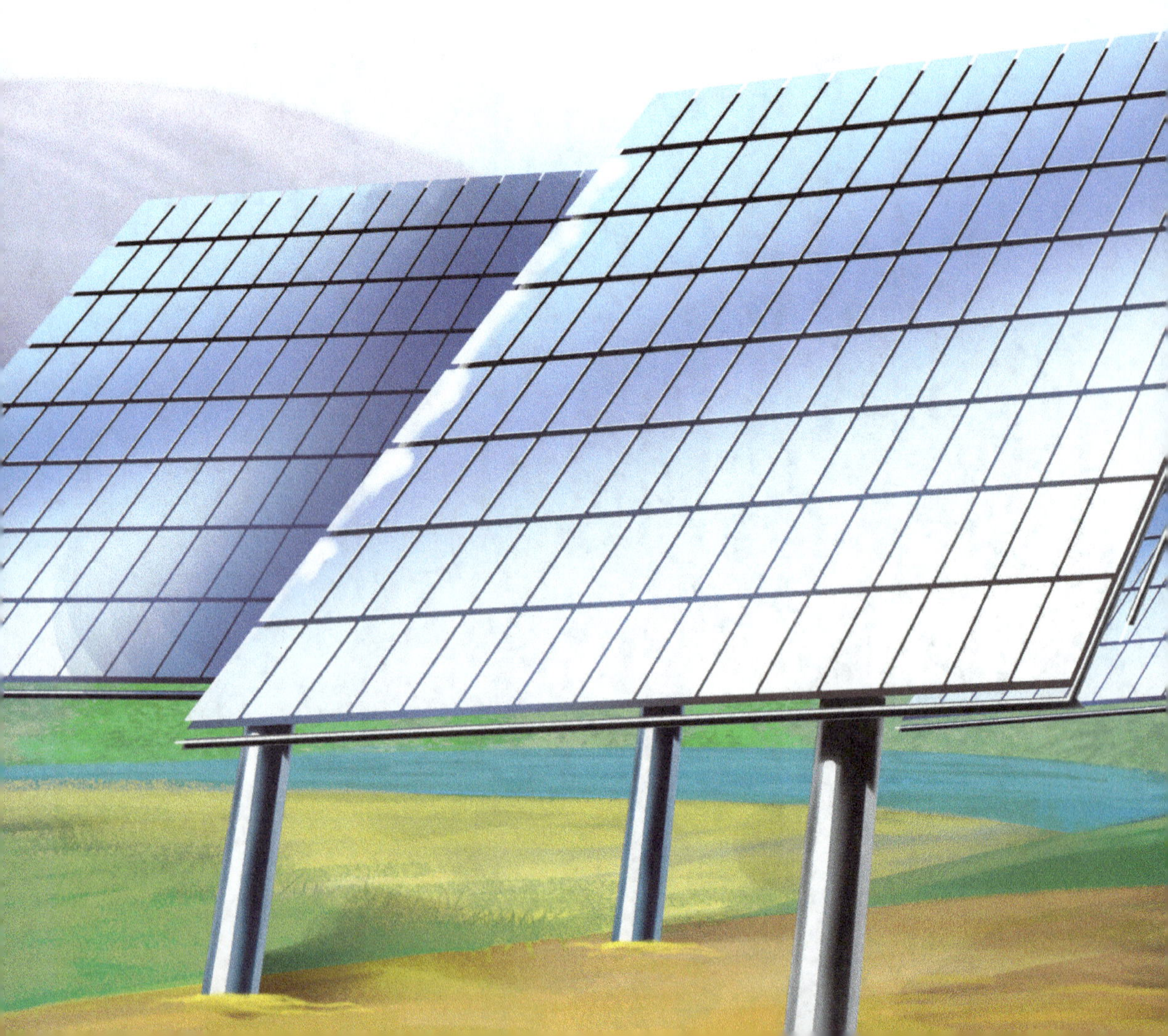

The knowledge power took care of education in the state. It was the basic power which further strengthened other powers. While the hydro-power gave new life to the famine-stricken Gujarat, the energy-power removed the poverty through providing much surplus power. Modi has not only succeeded in ushering an era of revolutionary development even in the corporate sector, he has succeeded in bringing out the white revolution. In fact these powers from the various sectors strengthened the very base of Modi's power. His energy rests on the people power of Gujarat.

Honour to Women

Narendra Modi always had much respect for women right from his early days. He has seen his mother getting exhausted with the domestic chores. His sister also helped her mother but still she needed an additional hand which was provided by the boy Modi. In order to lessen the domestic work's burden on his mother he always washed his own clothes and then himself ironed them. It was this sense of respect for the women which he depicted in his already referred play 'Peela Phool'. Most of the politicians regarded women as a mere support to men, although it is during Modi's regime that many women like Anandiben Patel, Smriti Irani, Sushma Swaraj could establish their distinct identity publicly.

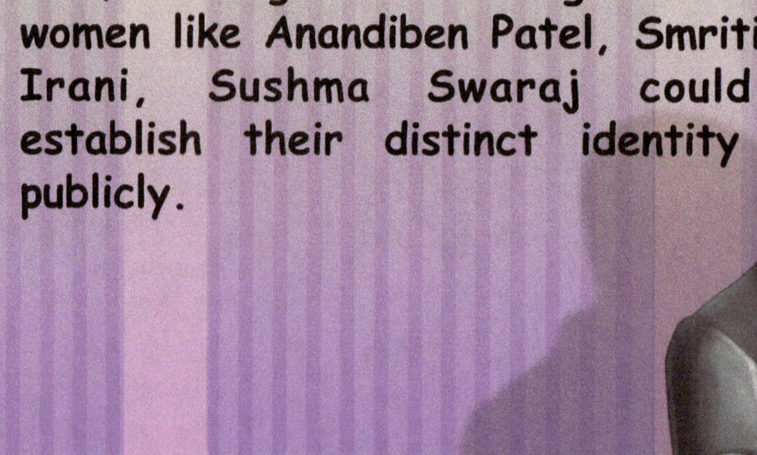

He wanted to empower women of Gujarat which was possible only through right kind of education. In order to ensure every girl to be educated, a free-education campaign, called ' Kanya Kelwaani ' (girl education) was launched in every school. For ensuring the presence of all the tribal girls in their classrooms, their parents were promised 40 kilo cereals gift in return, and this scheme proved very effective. Rupees two thousands were given to every girl student for buying a cycle if their school was 3 kms. away from their home. Free bus service, computer-training were provided and security bonds worth 1000 rupees were also distributed. For providing training to open home-industry units, many kitchen gardens were opened. Some mobile training centres were also opened.

Nationalism

Under his leadership Gujarat progressed in every field, so much so that the famous international magazines like 'Time' and ' Economic' praised profusely his development model. His perception of 'Hinduism' inspires the people to create an ideal state. He doesn't believe in any kind of discrimination and gives equal importance to everybody—whether one be a peasant or an officer. His mind has no room for any kind of caste-based orthodoxy. He deems country or nation to be supreme and nothing is above it. For Narendra Modi nationalism means development of all communities. He emphasizes the integrity of the nation. His religion is only 'India First' and the only holy book is the Indian Constitution.

Patriotism

The seed of patriotism took the root in his heart when he was hardly six years old. He was greatly impressed by the former Congress leader, Rasikbhai Dave, near whose office his father ran his tea-stall. Narendra would regularly visit the office of his role-model. When Rasikbhai started his campaign to make Gujarat a separate state, Narendra joined it enthusiastically.

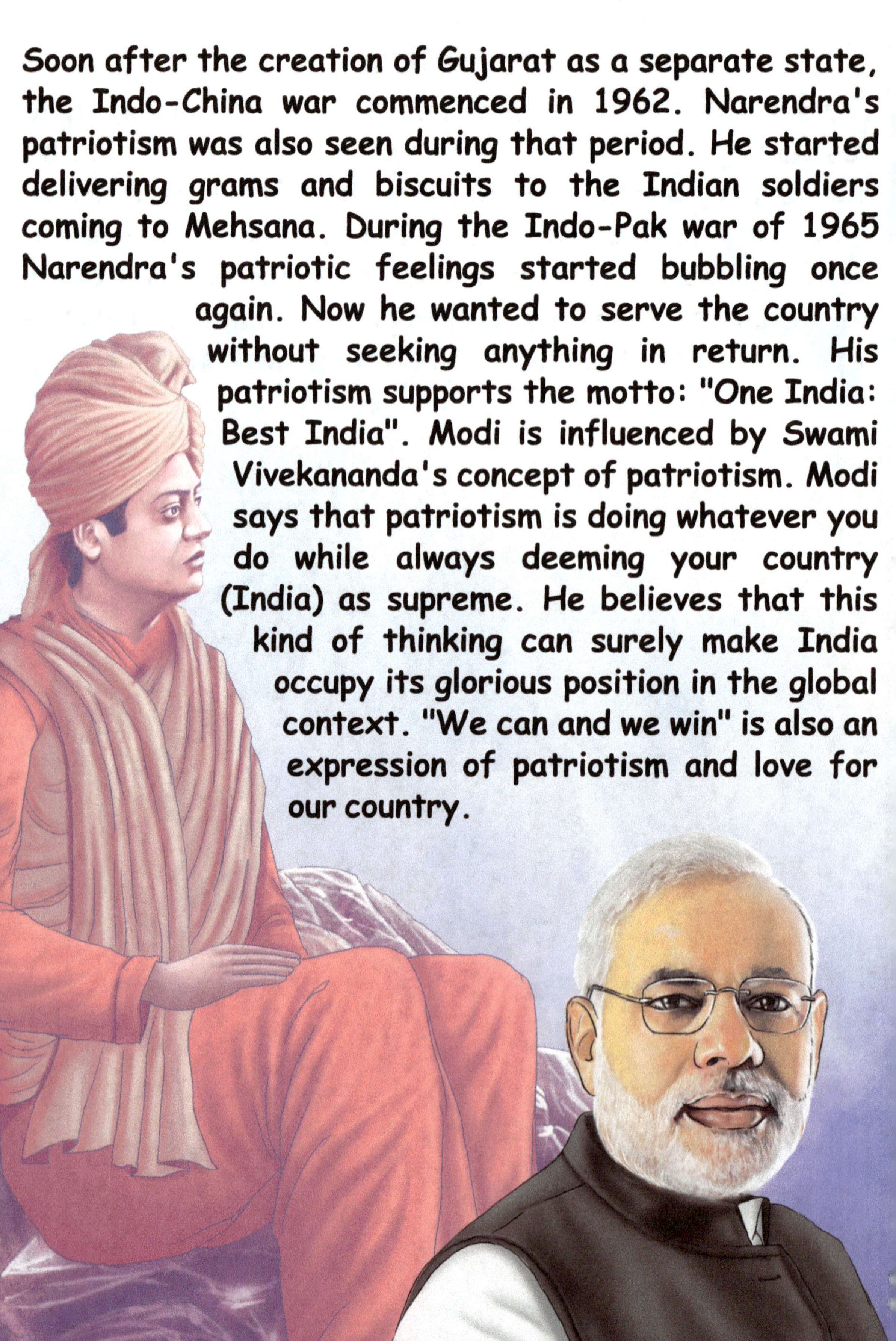

Soon after the creation of Gujarat as a separate state, the Indo-China war commenced in 1962. Narendra's patriotism was also seen during that period. He started delivering grams and biscuits to the Indian soldiers coming to Mehsana. During the Indo-Pak war of 1965 Narendra's patriotic feelings started bubbling once again. Now he wanted to serve the country without seeking anything in return. His patriotism supports the motto: "One India: Best India". Modi is influenced by Swami Vivekananda's concept of patriotism. Modi says that patriotism is doing whatever you do while always deeming your country (India) as supreme. He believes that this kind of thinking can surely make India occupy its glorious position in the global context. "We can and we win" is also an expression of patriotism and love for our country.

Role Model

So far the people of India had seen the persons of advanced age appearing as the leaders of the people. In such a common scenario, when Narendra Modi entered in the politics, his enchanting style of delivery of speech, dynamic personality and provoking thoughts gave a new ray of hope to the people of Gujarat. His impressive personality and fiery speeches received a warm welcome from the masses. He has become the role model of our country's youth.

Indian Development Schemes

The revolutionary development schemes launched and implemented by Prime Minister Shri Narendra Modi will help lead India towards the path of success by resolving economical conditions and reformation of various social issues. Because of this our country is being recognized world-over and their views are also changing towards our country.

Narendra Modi's Model of Development is highly praised across the nation. Introduction of revolutionary schemes such as Digital India, Clean India, Jan Dhan Yojna, Beti Padhao Beti Bachao, Make in India, Corruption Free India, and many more have changed the face of India. The country is being transformed into digital empowered society and knowledge economy. This initiative of e-governance and e-revolution aims at making all Government services accessible to the common man in his locality.

Pradhan Mantri Jan-Dhan Yojana (PMJDY), a National Mission for Financial Inclusion was introduced by the Prime Minister to ensure access to financial services, namely, Banking/ Savings & Deposit Accounts, Remittance, Credit, Insurance, Pension in an affordable manner. It was a grand success right from the day of inaugural. A record of 1.5 crore bank accounts were opened on the very first day across the country, the largest such exercise on a single day possibly anywhere in the world. So far, a total of more than 26 corers bank accounts are opened. Now common man will enjoy benefits of government schemes without having to go through endless waiting period or running from pillar to post. It will be reached directly to their accounts.

A nation which cannot ensure respect for its women, can never prosper. With the pet project launched by Prime Minister Shri Narender Modi "Beti bachao beti Padhao" (BBBP) Yojana (save daughter, educate daughter), countless girls and women have witnessed change in their lives. They are now making efforts towards fulfilling their dreams of being independent and having a career of their own.

India has the largest youth population in the world. With this in mind, Prime Minister Narendra Modi has taken a strong initiative named 'Make in India' project aiming at creating newer options and opportunities for employment in the country. In this way, our youth will develop his skills and contribute in the economy of the country.

India is an agrarian country. Our Pm Narendra Modi has introduced many new revolutionary schemes for the well being of agriculture sector in India. These plans have been introduced with an aim to ensure access to varied financial services including availability of basic savings bank account, remittances facility, access to need based credit, insurance and pension to the weaker sections, and low income groups. On the midnight of 9th November 2016, Shri Modi took a decision of demonetisation to curb the base of corruption in India. In this single move, he has attempted to tackle all major issues of the country including corruption, black money, terror funding, unemployment, and counterfeit currency in circulation. The impact of this great move has already started showing its results. All the schemes introduced by the Prime Minister are growth oriented and for the development of the country.